Deal with difficult people

How to cope with tricky situations in the workplace

A & C Black • London

Revised edition first published in Great Britain 2010

A & C Black Publishers Ltd
36 Soho Square
London W1D 3QY
www.acblack.com

A CIP record for this book is available from the British Library.

ISBN: 978–1–4081–2809–1

This book is produced using paper that is made from wood grown
in managed, sustainable forests. It is natural, renewable and
recyclable. The logging and manufacturing processes conform to
the environmental regulations of the country of origin.

Design by Fiona Pike, Pike Design, Winchester
Typeset by RefineCatch Limited, Bungay, Suffolk
Printed in Spain by GraphyCems

Contents

Handling office politics

Life would be wonderful if you could work in an office without worrying about other people and what they're up to. But everyone has a network of relationships throughout the organisation, and if you don't handle them carefully, you could be heading for an office nightmare.

You don't have to work somewhere long to work out whether or not is has a 'political' culture. In these organisations, *who* you know tends to matter more than *what* you know. Friendships and casual conversations take on a new significance — one wrong word to the wrong person could end up scuppering that promotion.

The context in which people have come to know each other is also important in a 'political' culture, as that can imply certain kinds of loyalty. Family, school, or social networks that intrude into professional territory can embroil people in all sorts of Machiavellian manoeuvrings that eventually create a politically charged workplace. If you find yourself in this sort of minefield, this chapter offers advice on how to pick your way through. It also suggests ways for managers to avoid and discourage 'politicking'.

Step one: Watch for signs of office politics

Politics plays a part in all organisations; it is an inevitable effect of putting human beings together in some sort of hierarchical arrangement. Indicators of office politics are often fairly easy to pick up—just hang around near the kettle, water cooler, or canteen in any organisation.

✔ Listen out for clues about how the business works under the surface. Perhaps you might hear comments from people who have been passed over for promotion in favour of the recruiting manager's former golf partner.

✔ Watch out for those who succeed by publicly supporting their boss, or by ensuring that they are always in the right place at the right time. Such successes again indicate that hidden agendas may be at play.

TOP TIP
If you're already embroiled in a political situation, it's important to go through the correct channels to avoid compromising yourself further. Explain what has happened to your supervisor or manager. If the political situation involves your boss, you may want to approach your human resources (HR) department, if you have one, to ask their advice about how to proceed.

Step two: Ensure your own survival

Self-preservation is always desirable, but don't use political dirty tricks to survive, whatever your level of responsibility— they will only create new nightmares. If your organisation is rife with politics, you can survive by following some simple rules.

✔ Observe the organisation's political style without getting involved until you're sure that you know what's going on. You may have started to notice coincidences or inconsistencies. Bide your time and watch the process so that you can begin to understand what the patterns and motivations are.

✔ Keep your own counsel during this period and work according to your own values; don't try to change your values to match those of the organisation; under pressure, your own values will reassert themselves forcefully. Remember that you just can't please everyone all the time, so use your own integrity to make decisions.

✔ Build a network of trusted allies. During your observation phase you will have identified who these people could be. It's also a good idea to build a network outside the organisation to create options and opportunities for yourself. This will take the focus off work for a while and gives you time to reconfirm or realign your values.

TOP TIP

Male networks have controlled the power in
businesses for hundreds of years and they are
almost impenetrable. If you are a woman in a
man's world, you may find it helpful to find a
mentor (male or female) inside or outside the
business, who will champion you and look
out for information and opportunities for you.
Build your relationships carefully and find
ways to contribute your skills and ideas that
will be valued by your male colleagues. Don't
let them take advantage of your talents,
though; follow up and ask for feedback.
In this way, you will build their respect
and find a tenable position amongst them.

✔ Expose other people's politically motivated behaviour.
When colleagues say one thing and do another, or seem
to be sabotaging your decisions or work relationships,
use your assertiveness skills to challenge their
motivation: 'You seem to be unhappy with the decisions
I've made; would you like to discuss them?' They will
either have to deny your assertion or confront it, but at
least the issue will be out in the open.

✔ Find a mentor with whom you can discuss your
observations and concerns. You may gain a deeper
understanding of the political processes at work and
some insight into how you can manage these more
effectively.

Step three: Discourage political behaviour

In any working environment, decision-making based on
politics will encourage hypocrisy, double-dealing, cliques,
self-interest, and deception. These must be reined in if the
business is going to survive in the long term. Here are a few
tips for those in managerial positions on how to create
change and avoid potential nightmares:

✔ Give promotions to the candidates who have
demonstrated a relevant track record of success.
Conduct structured, formal interviews and consult
with others affected by the decision. Match the
successful candidate to the job description. Remember

that although a good working relationship is necessary, the talents and values of the candidate don't have to match those of their new line manager exactly.

✓ Offer rewards and recognition solely for good performance, not in return for favours. All promotions or pay rises must be based on the individual's ability to reach or exceed the key performance indicators set during the performance review. Performance data should be available to those it concerns, with no hidden judgments or decisions.

✓ Communicate openly and transparently. Only unhealthy organisations hide information and spring unpleasant surprises on their employees. Communicate anything that affects your employees and their performance, including bad news, challenges, and initiatives for change.

✓ Introduce new initiatives, projects, and ideas on the basis of their value to the business, not on the basis of favouritism or possible personal benefit. Setting up a formal process for proposing new initiatives and tracing their evaluation and implementation will create confidence in an unbiased outcome.

✓ Don't be tempted to indulge in 'politicking', even when you can see an opportunity to benefit either yourself or the organisation as a whole. For example, you might want to offload a member of your team in order to attract someone you feel may perform more effectively.

However, this is where the rot sets in. If you manage people on this basis, you will destroy any trust your team has in you and their performance may deteriorate.

Common mistakes

✗ **You misread a situation and wade in with an accusation of politicking**
At best this reveals your naïvety, at worst your own politicking or neuroses. If you think a colleague is politically motivated, observe the person's behaviour until you're sure that you understand it. You may wish to share your thoughts with someone you trust or, if it serves a purpose, confront the situation. Sometimes it's best to leave things alone. You will be the best judge of this.

✗ **You build a network purely for your own ends**
Some people try to short-circuit the path to promotion by cultivating what they believe to be essential relationships. However, there is a big difference between building professional networks and using your contacts shamelessly in a headlong pursuit of your own selfish ends. Remember that if you launch yourself into an early promotion without having developed the skills to be successful, you may be setting yourself up for a very public and career-damaging failure. Build your networks prudently and use them to help develop your skills and deliver new opportunities. It may take a little longer, but it will pay off in the end.

✗ You get involved in the politics too early

When you join a new organisation, try not to get bogged down with the politics at an early stage. Make the most of your first few weeks in your new job: your newness in the business will allow you to ask naïve questions that will help you create a picture of the political environment. Keep your relationships open and friendly and build your network with a diverse range of people. Observe the patterns of relationships closely to see where the information lies and where the power sits. After a few months you will probably have acquired a fairly accurate idea of what is going on. You are then in a position to be able to make your own decisions about the extent to which you should get involved in organisational politics.

✗ You communicate badly

Poor communication within an organisation is probably the most common cause of a destructive political culture. In the absence of sufficient information or an adequate explanation, people will fill the gaps with speculation and rumour, which circulate around the office grapevine very fast. Clear and transparent communication, leaving people in no doubt about plans or decisions, helps protect an organisation from becoming a breeding ground for politics. Newsletters, bulletin boards on an intranet, and company-wide meetings are all useful vehicles for disseminating information, along with more local activities such as team meetings, departmental get-togethers, and personal briefings.

STEPS TO SUCCESS

✔ Listen out for signs of political machinations. Informal situations can be the most fruitful for this kind of research.

✔ Communicate openly and transparently in order to discourage gossip and encourage trust.

✔ Don't be tempted into politicking—it's unlikely to end well. Keep out of it and keep your integrity.

✔ Build a network of trusted allies and confidants, both inside and outside the organisation.

✔ If you must confront a political situation, go through formal channels so that your position isn't compromised.

✔ Try not to get involved until you fully understand all aspects of the conflict.

Useful links

iVillage office politics:
**www.ivillage.co.uk/workcareer/survive/archive/
0,,156475,00.html**
Prospects:
**www.prospects.ac.uk/p/articles/win_at_office_politics.
jsp**
MindTools:
www.mindtools.com/pages/article/newCDV_85.htm

Coping with a difficult boss

Many people have a difficult or challenging relationship with their boss. It can be tempting to lay the blame for this type of situation at the boss's feet due to his or her unreasonable, negative, awkward, or unhelpful behaviour. Whether blaming your boss is justified or not, the good news is that, as a significant party in the relationship, there is a great deal that you can do to end the bad boss nightmare.

Step one: Consider the impact on your own health and happiness

Rather than deal with the problem directly, many people are tempted to live with the difficulties of having a troublesome boss. Instead of addressing the problem, they brush it under the carpet by looking for ways of minimising the impact he or she has on their working lives. However, employing avoidance tactics or finding ways to offset the emotional damage can be time-consuming and stressful.

Focusing on your own wellbeing may encourage you to tackle the issue rationally and try to reach a sensible accommodation that will prevent you from jeopardising your health or feeling that you have to leave your job.

Step two: Understand your boss

When you come to look more closely at your relationship with your boss, the first thing to do is to realise how much of it is due to the structure of the organisation—for example, your boss necessarily has to give you tasks, some of which you may not enjoy—and how much is due to truly unreasonable behaviour.

Looking at the wider issues in the organisation may provide the key to the problem. 'Difficult boss syndrome' is rarely caused simply by a personality clash: more often than not, there are broader organisational factors that can go some way to explaining seemingly unreasonable behaviour.

✔ However uncomfortable it may feel, try putting yourself in your boss's shoes. Recognise the objectives that define his or her role and think through the pressures they are under.

✔ Make a mental list of your boss's strengths, preferred working style, idiosyncrasies, values, and beliefs. Observe his or her behaviour and reactions, and watch where he or she chooses to focus attention.

This will help you deepen your understanding. Very often, when we feel disliked or when we dislike someone, we avoid building this understanding and instead look for ways of avoiding the issues.

TOP TIP

If your boss is making work intolerable
because of his or her moody and bad-
tempered behaviour, try to work out how you
could influence the situation for the better.
Observe his or her behaviour to see if there
is a pattern in it, and then try to broach this
issue by letting your boss know how his or
her mood swings affect you. Use assertive
language and ask if there is anything you
can do to alleviate the cause of the problem.
If the behaviour persists, consult your
human resources department to see if
there are any formal procedures in
place to deal with such a situation.

Step three: Compare the way you both perceive your role

As part of the process of understanding your boss, compare
the perceptions you both have of your role and the criteria
used to judge your success. You may feel that you're
performing well, but if you're putting your energy into tasks
that your boss does not feel are relevant, you will be seen
as performing poorly.

✔ Take the initiative to explore your boss's expectations
   and agree on your objectives. This will clarify your role

and give you a better idea of how to progress in the organisation.

TOP TIP

A lack of communication often contributes to workplace misunderstandings. If you feel like you're missing out on opportunities or being denied information because you're not one of your boss's favourites, try approaching him or her with information about what you're doing and talk about your methods and goals. If your boss persists in denying you the information you need, you may have a case of bullying against him or her.

Step four: Understand yourself

Having scrutinised your boss and developed a greater understanding of him or her, you should try doing the same exercise on yourself. Sometimes, a lack of self-knowledge leads to us being surprised by our reactions and the feedback we get. Ask for input from your colleagues while you're doing this.

✔ Ask your colleagues what they observe when you interact with your boss, how you come across to them, and how you could manage your communication differently. Although their perception may not represent the absolute truth about you, it nonetheless reflects the image you create.

✔ Think through some of the past encounters you've had with your boss and reflect upon them objectively, perhaps with a friend or colleague who knows you well. Maybe this situation happens over and over again, which suggests that you harbour a value or belief that is being repeatedly compromised. If you can understand what this is, you can learn to manage these situations more effectively.

✔ Consider changing some of your behaviour. This often prompts a reciprocal behavioural change in your boss. If you don't change anything about the way you interact with your boss, the relationship will remain unaltered, so this is definitely worth a try.

For example, perhaps you value attention to detail, but your boss is a big-picture person. Every time you ask for more detailed information, you will be drawing attention to one of your boss's vulnerabilities, and he or she is likely to become unco-operative or irritated by your request. Once you've observed your respective patterns, you can begin to work around them or accommodate them.

Step five: Remember that the relationship is mutual

In order to be effective, managers need a co-operative and productive team. But in order to be part of such a team, each member needs their manager to provide the resources and support they need to do their job properly. An unsupportive boss can be just as nightmarish as a vindictive one.

When managers neglect to give their employees the information and feedback they need, employees are forced to second-guess their boss's requirements. This inevitably leads to misunderstandings on both sides. The knock-on effects of this are an atmosphere of distrust and ill-will, and mutual recriminations—not to mention the negative impact on the organisation's productivity levels.

✔ Ask for the information and resources you require, or find other ways to get these, as this will put you in control of the situation and protect you from the need to improvise.

Nightmare situations can arise when employees' needs aren't met. Some people become angry and resentful of the manager's authority; some find ways of challenging decisions in order to assert their own power; and others develop agendas of their own that are neither helpful nor productive.

One-sided relationships are a recipe for revolution! It is rare in business to find relationships where there is absolutely *no* reciprocal power. Remember that if you're no longer willing to spend time managing your difficult boss, you still have the ultimate power: you can just walk away.

TOP TIP

If your boss is making you feel miserable by
constantly making negative and derisive
comments about the way you do your work,
you need to find a private moment when you
can explain how this makes you feel and ask
your boss to stop doing it. You could suggest
that he or she gives you clear guidelines
and constructive feedback that will help
you to meet his or her expectations and
develop your talents. Point out that constant
nagging affects the way you work and
that you would be much more effective
if he or she took a positive interest in
what you do. If the negativity continues,
you may decide to lodge a complaint of
discrimination against your boss. If you
take this route, make sure you have a
record of the incidents and a note of any
witnesses present. Also seek further
advice from your human resources
department if your company has one.

Common mistakes

✗ **You take your boss's behaviour personally**
It is very tempting to take the behaviour of a difficult
boss personally. However, it is very unlikely that *you*
are the problem. It may be something you do, it may

be the values you hold, or it may be that you remind your boss of someone he or she doesn't get on with. The only person who loses out if you take it personally is you.

✗ You don't remain detached

Many difficult relationships deteriorate to the point where they are fraught with contempt and confrontation. This is never helpful in a work setting and only makes matters uncomfortable for everyone. If you find yourself being drawn into an angry exchange, try to remain emotionally detached and listen actively to what is being said to (or shouted at) you. It may provide you with clues about why the situation has developed and allow you to get straight to the point of concern. Ask for a private review afterwards to explore the incident when feelings aren't running so high. You may find that this brings to the surface issues that are relatively easy to deal with and that will prevent further outbursts from occurring.

✗ You never confront the issue

Facing up to difficult people is not an easy thing to do and so many people avoid biting the bullet. However, this will only prolong a miserable situation. Acquiescence enables bullying to thrive and allows the aggressors to hold power. Break the cycle by taking responsibility for your share of the problem and examining what it is you're doing to provoke conflict between you and your boss. Doing nothing is not a viable option.

STEPS TO SUCCESS

✔ Don't neglect the problem—for the sake of your health, if nothing else.

✔ Try to see both sides of the issue.

✔ Ask for impartial help from colleagues if you feel too emotionally involved.

✔ Identify and resolve areas of ambiguity in order to reduce the possibility of misunderstandings and dissatisfaction.

✔ Don't take it personally . . .

✔ . . . but remember that you might need to change too.

Useful links

Bully Online:
www.bullyonline.org
TUC:
www.tuc.org.uk/tuc/rights_bullyatwork.cfm
National Bullying Helpline:
www.nationalbullyinghelpline.co.uk
Directgov:
www.direct.gov.org.uk/en/employment/resolving workplacedisputes/discriminationatwork/ DG_10026670

Dealing with bullying or harassment

Anyone who has ever been bullied will know just how demoralising and damaging the experience can be. When it occurs in the workplace it can be a seemingly inescapable nightmare. The effects of bullying impact on a person's life outside of work and are sure to take their toll over time on both the physical and mental wellbeing of the victim.

Abusive behaviours range from the extreme, such as bullying and physical abuse, to more subtle forms of harassment that are often more common but less recognised. What is tolerated in the workplace will depend very much upon the culture of the organisation and the attitudes of its leaders.

Some businesses ignore all forms of harassment; others make a point of creating a culture where intimidation of any sort is cause for reprimand or, in some cases, dismissal. It is worth reflecting on your organisation's culture to see what exists, both on and under the surface. This chapter provides advice both for the victims of harassment or bullying and the colleagues and managers around them.

Step one: Understand the forms bullying can take

The recipient of bullying is often in a weaker position, physically, emotionally, or hierarchically. Victims are usually unable or unwilling to stand up for themselves, due to what they feel will be the unacceptable consequences, such as an escalation of abusive behaviour or the threat of redundancy. This fear allows the behaviour to continue.

Any form of harassment can have a serious impact on the morale of staff in the business, and can affect the performance and health of individuals. Not only is it simply wrong, but it's unlawful, and should be treated seriously.

Different forms of harassment

These include:

- all manner of physical contact from touching, pushing, and shoving, to serious assault
- intrusive or obsessive behaviours, such as constant pestering, baiting, or dogging a person's movements
- tricks being played that result in risk or danger to the individual
- group bullying, where the individual is overpowered by a number of aggressors

Less direct harassment may include:

- the spreading of rumours, jokes, or offensive personal remarks
- written statements, letters, or graffiti
- actions that isolate the individual and prevent them from doing their work effectively
- non-co-operation, or sabotage of professional objectives
- pressure for sexual favours
- obscene gestures and comments
- the orchestration of situations that compromise the individual
- manipulative 'political' behaviours, that may include bribery or blackmail

TOP TIP

The difference between a good joke and bullying can be a subtle one that isn't always immediately noticeable. A good joke contributes to a fun atmosphere at work, and can diffuse a tense situation—but it needs to be a joke that everyone finds amusing, and isn't at someone else's expense. However, if the joke involves a person in the office being demeaned or belittled in any way, it has gone too far. Similarly a joke that is personally critical and destructive has also crossed the line.

Step two: Determine when the line has been crossed

Often, people find it hard to know whether the line of harassment has been crossed. If they confront the perpetrators, they can be accused of 'being a poor sport', or worse. Such accusations are often levelled to mask what is going on, and can seriously undermine the victim's confidence.

If you are the one being bullied, the following advice will help you determine whether the harassment is trivial or serious:

✔ Seek feedback from those who may have observed any incidents. Their objectivity will help put perspective on the situation if you're worried that you may be over-reacting. It may be that their account gives you more ammunition to deal with the problem appropriately. Select your witness carefully though—ones you can trust to be allies throughout the ordeal, who won't 'flip' on you under pressure.

✔ If the harassment is infrequent and seems harmless, try not to take it too personally. Bullying says more about the character of the bully than it does about the person being bullied. However, if the bullying is persistent or escalates, you must confront it and report it. Even if you don't wish to face the bully head on, there are likely to be other ways of asserting your rights.

TOP TIP
If you feel you're being bullied, but the
perpetrator disguises his or her actions in
jest, one way of dealing with this is to write
down the incidents in a journal, including
the context in which they took place. Ask
for feedback from observers and include
their comments. Over time, you will be
able to see if there is a pattern to the
treatment you've been receiving.
Also, the record may be useful if you
decide to take the matter further.

✔ Check in the employees' handbook, if you have one.
There are probably procedures in place to assist you in
dealing with your situation. You may be advised to report
the incident(s) to your manager but, should you feel
uncomfortable about this—for example, if your manager
is part of the problem—you may wish to go directly to
the human resources department.

✔ If you decide to lodge a formal complaint, make sure you
have a record of the incidents and a note of the
witnesses present.

TOP TIP
If you see a colleague being bullied and no
complaint is forthcoming, you may think
about intervening at an informal level. Start
by asking your harassed colleague about the

treatment they received. The person may indicate that they don't want to make a fuss about it and will leave it at that. Alternatively, you could speak to the bully, explaining the impact of their behaviour on the team as a whole. When doing this, use good feedback techniques. For example, begin all your statements with 'I . . . ', and base them on events that you have personally observed.

Step three: Maintain a non-bullying atmosphere

Left unchecked, bullying can destroy the morale of valued employees and put the surrounding people into a state of fear. If you're a manager, you have a responsibility to report bullying elsewhere in the organisation, even if it doesn't affect your staff. However, you don't want to create an atmosphere of persecution either. Try to strike a balance between vigilance and freedom of choice.

✔ Bear in mind your legal obligations to your staff. Remember that turning a blind eye to the problem may at some point make you culpable as well.

✔ Reassure staff that their complaints will be taken seriously and dealt with fairly. Most people are reluctant to report harassment because of the potential impact on their position/job. Explain what steps have to be taken, and estimate the length of time involved in the process.

✔ Give any potential complainant a few days in which to reconsider making a formal complaint. Don't exert pressure to take the issue further if the recipient decides to let the matter go—it's his or her choice and this should be respected.

✔ Make sure that the organisation's policy manual spells out how to proceed if the person decides to pursue the charge. It will probably involve investigating the details to establish what happened, and in what context. This may involve interviews with the victim, alleged abuser, and witnesses. Notes—based on facts, not hearsay and opinions—should be taken and filed with the human resources department or representative.

Cases of serious assault are rare, but when they occur, they may go beyond the scope of the organisation to deal with them. It may be necessary to contact a security officer or the police, and you may also need medical intervention and/or counselling for the victim, perhaps the perpetrator, and even some affected colleagues.

The incident could also involve an external third party, such as a customer. It is important to have a plan in place for such events, and then react in as calm and professional a manner as possible. The more serious the problem, the more your employees will depend on you to bring the matter to a close as quickly and judiciously as you can. Minimising 'collateral damage' helps restore equilibrium more quickly.

TOP TIP
Once someone's confidence has been broken, they become 'easy pickings' and can inadvertently encourage bullying behaviours. If this is the case, you should still approach the victim and express your concern. If the problem persists, you would be wise to raise the issue in a staff meeting, or to report it to the person's supervisor—or to another manager of equal or greater rank.

Common mistakes

✗ **You act before you know all the facts**
Wading in with accusations when you think you've witnessed an episode of bullying could make matters worse: you may have misjudged the situation. Unless it's a serious incident, it's best to observe and question before intervening. In this way, all parties are given a chance to explain their behaviour and resolve the situation calmly.

✗ **You mistake a genuine extrovert for a bully**
Extroverts frequently speak their minds before really thinking about what they are saying—which can sound confrontational and be mistaken for harassment. Being

extroverts, however, they are often receptive to questioning and keen to point out that they were just testing the boundaries, or joking. By sharing your perception and inviting theirs, it's possible to clarify and dispel the situation without further entanglement.

✗ You don't consider that the bully may need help too

It is easy to assume that bullies are strong characters. Indeed, it's often to create this impression that they become bullies in the first place. In fact, most bullies are insecure and behave as they do to mask a lack of knowledge or skill. Or perhaps they are mirroring behaviour further up the organisation, thinking that this may help them advance. One way of handling such a person is to offer them coaching, so that they can be helped to understand the underlying cause, and succeed in changing their behaviour.

STEPS TO SUCCESS

✔ Be aware that there are many kinds of bullying. You may be suffering in more ways than you know.

✔ Ask others for their opinions on whether the way you've been treated constitutes bullying.

✔ If the line has been crossed, resolve to take action and assert your rights.

✔ Try to go through formal, established channels rather than confronting the issue on your own.

✔ As a manager, take responsibility for eliminating harassment in whichever department you witness it.

✔ Make it known that bullying is not to be tolerated and that complaints will be dealt with fairly.

✔ Try to have procedures in place to deal with every eventuality.

✔ Do not force people to complain if they would rather not.

Useful links

Acas (Advisory, Conciliation and Arbitration Service):
www.acas.org.uk/index.aspx?articleid=794
Bully Online:
www.bullyonline.org/workbully/index.htm
TUC:
www.tuc.org.uk/tuc/rights_bullyatwork.cfm
National Bullying Helpline:
www.nationalbullyinghelpline.co.uk

Dealing with discrimination against you

Discrimination against individuals on the basis of their race, ethnic background, sex, sexual orientation, marital or civil partnership status, pregnancy or maternity leave, gender reassignment, age, religion or belief, or physical/mental impairment is unlawful. Such individuals are also protected against harassment or victimisation at work.

However, not all employers obey the rules and enforcing the law can be a nightmare in itself. The Equality Act 2010, which is due to come into effect in October 2010, aims to simplify existing anti-discrimination measures for individuals and will make it much easier for them to bring complaints of discrimination.

The laws against discrimination at work cover every part of employment, which includes recruitment, terms and conditions, pay and benefits, status, training, promotion and transfer opportunities, right through to redundancy and dismissal.

Discrimination can be direct or indirect:

- *Direct* discrimination is when a person in one of the above groups is treated less favourably at work than another, such as a female employee being paid less than a male colleague for doing the same job.
- *Indirect* discrimination is when a working condition or rule disadvantages one group of people more than another, such as introducing a dress code without good reason, which might discriminate against some ethnic groups.

What is positive action?

An employer may offer extra support specifically to men or women, or to a particular racial group, by way of training or encouragement to apply for certain jobs, in order to redress an imbalance in the workforce. This is known as 'positive action'. However, when choosing who is to fill a post, the employer must consider all candidates on merit alone. From October 2010, the use of positive action will be extended to include the recruitment process, so that, when faced with two equally qualified individuals for a job, an employer will be allowed to favour a candidate from an under-represented group.

In a few cases, a job offer may be restricted to a particular group if there is a genuine occupational requirement. This could include:

- some jobs in single-sex or religious schools
- jobs in organisations based on a religious or belief ethos
- jobs in some welfare services or charities that provide support to a particular group
- acting jobs that require a man or woman, or someone from a particular racial background or of a certain age

Everyone has an equal right to employment with fair remuneration in an environment that is free from discrimination. There are few experiences more depressing than being treated unfairly because of who you are. Fortunately, there are established ways in which you can tackle any type of discrimination.

Discrimination is a huge subject, and there are many resources you can turn to if you feel that you've been discriminated against. However, the following will provide a useful starting point. More information can be found using the extensive links at the end of the chapter.

Step one: Racial discrimination

If you feel you've been discriminated against because of your race, colour, nationality or ethnic background, don't wait; there are time limits for bringing a case under the Race Relations Act. A complaint about race discrimination in employment must be brought to an employment tribunal within three months of the act complained of.

✓ Gather as much evidence as possible and create a good record of the incident(s) along with a list of any witnesses. Racial discrimination isn't easy to prove and the burden of proof will be on you.

✓ Seek guidance from trusted friends and professional confidants at the earliest opportunity and explore the legal assistance that you may be eligible for. You can go to your union, the Citizens Advice Bureau, or the Equality and Human Rights Commission.

Step two: Sex discrimination

The Sex Discrimination Act 1975 makes it unlawful for employers to discriminate on the grounds of gender, sexuality, marital status, or gender reassignment.

If you were dismissed for poor performance while a poorly performing colleague of the opposite gender retained their job, you may have a claim for sex discrimination. If you were selected for redundancy, you may have a claim if you can show that the selection criteria used affected one sex more than the other with no rational justification.

Step three: Sexual orientation discrimination

The Employment Equality (Sexual Orientation) Regulations 2003 prohibit discrimination on the grounds of sexual orientation. You are protected against sexual orientation discrimination if:

- you are lesbian, gay, bisexual or heterosexual
- people think you are gay, lesbian or heterosexual when you are not
- you have gay friends or visit gay clubs

If you're a same-sex couple in a civil partnership, you are entitled to the same benefits as a married person (for example, survivors' benefits under a company pension scheme, or cover provided by a company's private healthcare scheme) if the benefits have been in place since 5 December 2005 (when the Civil Partnership Act came into force).

If your employer gives benefits to unmarried partners of its employees, such as permission to drive the company car, then refusing the same benefits to same-sex partners could be discrimination.

Step four: Equal pay

The issue of pay within the area of sex discrimination is covered specifically by the Equal Pay Act 1970. The Equal Pay Act does not cover you for being treated differently to members of the same sex, only the opposite sex. However, because the majority of part-timers still tend to be women, there is also a clause relating to the rights of part-timers.

There are two ways of looking at equal pay. Sometimes a person is paid less than a colleague of the opposite sex for doing the same job. Other times, one individual is paid less than another of the opposite sex for doing work of equivalent value.

Both these situations are discriminatory and may be unlawful. Equal pay rights apply to both sexes. Equal pay legislation extends beyond just wages and salaries; it also covers bonuses, benefits, overtime, holiday pay, sick pay, performance-related pay, and occupational pensions.

Examples of pay discrimination

There are several ways in which pay discrimination can take place. Here are some examples:

- A woman is appointed on a lower salary than her male counterparts.
- A woman on maternity leave is denied a bonus received by other staff.
- The jobs that women occupy are given different job titles and grades to those of male colleagues doing virtually the same work.
- Part-time staff have no entitlement to sick pay or holiday pay.
- All staff are placed on individual contracts and not allowed to discuss their pay rates.

Your rights to equal pay are set out in the Equal Pay Act 1970 (see www.eoc-law.org.uk). You can take your claim for equal pay to an employment tribunal at any time while you're in the job, or within six months of leaving employment.

TOP TIP

It may be that a colleague of the opposite sex to you has been receiving superior benefits, despite doing the same job and to the same standard. Equal pay law embraces benefits, bonuses, pensions, holiday, and sick pay as well as salary. If you can prove that your job is comparable to a colleague's, involving the same level of skills and knowledge, then you're likely to have a case. However, you must be able to demonstrate this before you proceed to a tribunal with your claim.

Step five: Sexual harassment

The Sex Discrimination Act makes it unlawful for employers to treat a woman less favourably than a man (or a man less favourably than a woman) by subjecting her or him to any emotional or physical harm. The Act also applies to individuals undergoing gender reassignment.

You can only make a claim if the incident(s) took place at work or at a work-related function. Sexual harassment is defined as unwelcome physical, verbal, or non-verbal conduct of a sexual nature. Cases are most likely to be brought as civil claims in an employment tribunal.

Examples of sexual harassment at work

These include:

- Requests or demands for sexual favours by either gender.
- Comments about your appearance which are derisory or demeaning.
- Remarks that are designed to cause offence.
- Intrusive questions or speculations about your sex life.
- Any behaviour related to gender that creates an intimidating, hostile, or humiliating working environment.

Incidents involving touching or more extreme physical threats are criminal offences and should be reported to the police as well as your employer.

TOP TIP
If your boss has made even a single sexual advance on you, you may have grounds for a complaint. You don't have to experience

**persistent sexual harassment before you ask
for help—if it's sufficiently serious, one
incident can amount to sex discrimination.
However, before you start down this road,
think about taking your complaint to the
human resources department or to a trusted
superior to see if there are any internal
policies that can support or protect you and
help to resolve the situation.**

Step six: Disability discrimination

If you're disabled, or have had a disability, the Disability
Discrimination Act (DDA) makes it unlawful for you to be
discriminated against in the areas of:

- employment
- access to goods, facilities, and services
- the management, buying, or renting of land or property

The DDA was passed in 1995 (and extended by the
Disability Discrimination Act 2005) to introduce new
measures aimed at ending the discrimination which many
disabled people face in these areas. It uses the term
'disability' to describe 'anyone with a physical or mental
impairment which has a substantial and long-term adverse
effect upon their ability to carry out normal day-to-day
activities'.

Your employer has a duty to make 'reasonable adjustments'

to make sure you're not put at a substantial disadvantage by employment arrangements or any physical feature of the workplace. These could include:

- making physical adjustments to the premises
- supplying special equipment to help you do your job
- altering your hours of work or giving you extra time off for assessment, treatment or rehabilitation
- providing training or retraining if you cannot do your current job any longer
- transferring you to a different post or workplace

From October 2010 it will be unlawful for an employer to ask job-seekers invasive questions about disability and health before the job offer stage (unless intrinsically necessary for the role). Once an individual has received a job offer, an employer can ask these questions, in order to consider whether any specific adaptations will be necessary. However, if an individual finds that his or her job offer is withdrawn after such a disclosure, he or she will have a claim and the onus will be on the employer to prove that this was not due to discrimination.

TOP TIP

Your employer shouldn't discriminate against you because you've taken a case of discrimination to a tribunal. People who helped you by providing evidence or information are also protected from such discrimination.

Step seven: Ageism

The Equality (Age) Regulations 2006 provide protection against age discrimination in employment, training and adult education. Discrimination can be direct or indirect and is unlawful unless the employer can justify the discrimination or if an exception applies. The Regulations over age discrimination in most aspects of employment include:

- recruitment and job applications
- training and development
- redundancy and dismissal
- retirement

Examples of ageism in the workplace

These include:

- A person is refused a job because they are over a certain age.
- Promotions to senior positions are only given to people under a certain age.
- Recruitment notices or advertisements that stipulate 'recent graduate' – few older people would be able to meet this requirement.
- An older employee is refused the same training as younger employees.

A company may discriminate on the grounds of age in a number of cases

These include:

- where existing law stipulates an age requirement, e.g. an employee must be over 18 to serve alcohol
- where there is a genuine occupation requirement, e.g. for an actor for a role needs to be a particular age
- where the employer relies on the National Minimum Wage for young people

It is worth checking out the Code of Practice using the links at the end of this chapter. It can be a valuable yardstick for judging your organisation's policies.

Step eight: Religion or belief discrimination

The Employment Equality (Religion or Belief) Regulations 2003 make it unlawful for employers to discriminate on the grounds of religion or a religious or philosophical belief. This includes all major religions as well as less practised ones. Political beliefs do not count. The Equality Act 2006 extended protection to those who do not follow any religion or belief.

Under the Regulations your employer is not obliged to give you time off or provide facilities for religious observance in the workplace, but should try to do so where possible, provided it does not disrupt others or your ability to do your job properly. If you want time off for religious holidays, your employer should consider your request sympathetically but they can refuse if it will affect the business.

Your employer may be at risk of indirect discrimination if they impose a working condition or rule which disadvantages people of a particular religion or belief. For instance:

- Running a regular training seminar on Friday afternoons could disadvantage individuals of certain faiths for whom Friday is an important religious day.
- Introducing a dress code may discriminate against individuals who wear certain clothing or jewellery for religious reasons.

Indirect discrimination is not always unlawful, but for it to be justified an employer would have to show there was a real business need, or a health and safety risk, and that there was no alternative.

If you think you have been discriminated against because of your religion or belief (or lack of one), try talking to your employer or your human resources department first. Or you can seek advice from your union, the Citizens Advice Bureau, or the Equality and Human Rights Commission. In some cases you can apply to an employment tribunal to decide if you are being discriminated against for your religion or belief (or lack of one).

Common mistakes

✗ You rush into litigation

In all cases except racial discrimination (where there's a time limit), rushing into making a claim is a mistake. The process of taking action is lengthy and evidence needs to be produced to back up your claim. Even when this is available, the procedures are stressful and time consuming. It is always best to see if you can find another way around the problem. Start by broaching the subject with the perpetrator or having a discussion with the human resources department or an external source of advice.

✗ You're not sure of your ground

Misunderstanding a situation or someone's behaviour can lead to false claims of discrimination. It's important to be sure of your facts and do the research necessary to back them up. Although you'll have to talk with colleagues and perhaps consult with others in the organisation, do this confidentially to avoid drawing attention to a situation that may not develop into a claim.

✗ You think that office parties don't count

It's a mistake to think that being 'off duty' or away from the work premises with your colleagues protects you from being accused of harassment. Under the Sex Discrimination Act, sex discrimination is outlawed in a wide variety of contexts that are related to your employment. In certain circumstances, action can be taken if it can be shown that the (social) event at which the incident occurred was linked to your employment.

STEPS TO SUCCESS

✔ Be aware of your rights. Check out the law using the links below or by contacting an independent body.

✔ Before you take action, consult the appropriate authorities within and outside your organisation.

✔ Collect documentary evidence and witnesses to support your claims.

✔ Explore alternatives to legal action before rushing into making a claim.

✔ Be prepared for a lengthy process if you take your complaint to a tribunal. This course of action can be stressful and expensive, so make sure you use it only as a last resort.

Useful links

Citizens Advice:
www.citizensadvice.org.uk
Directgov:
www.direct.gov.uk/en/employment/resolvingwork placedisputes/discriminationatwork/DG_443

Preventing discrimination

The cost of claims being brought by employees against their employers is rising. In the United Kingdom over 150,000 employment tribunal claims were accepted in 2008/9, a decrease of 20% from 2007/8 but an increase of 14% from 2006/7.

This statistic should prevent any employer from thinking that it couldn't happen to them. For the small to medium-sized business, who may not be insured against such eventualities, litigation has been known to jeopardise their future viability and, in some cases, has resulted in the business closing entirely.

This chapter offers advice to managers and employers on how to avoid this nightmare by preventing discriminatory practices from entering the workplace.

Step one: Educate your employees

All employees must be aware of discriminatory issues, and if you are a manager, it's your responsibility to make sure that all relevant information is available, that best practice is encouraged, and that diversity is valued. The senior

managers should set the tone for this environment and
their actions should exemplify the culture you want.

✔ Publish your policy on discrimination prominently in
the workplace and on your company intranet, if you
have one.

✔ Establish processes that will encourage the fair
treatment of everyone in the organisation, and review
your progress regularly.

✔ Use every opportunity to publicise your policy,
and include a clear statement of it in all company
literature.

✔ Be seen to implement the policy so that your employees
have faith in its authority and effectiveness.

Step two: Implement the right procedures

A discrimination-free working environment should have the
following policies and procedures in place:

■ Policies and decision-making processes that are
transparent so that there are no misunderstandings
when decisions made *apparently* discriminate against
someone on the basis of their gender, sexual preference,
race, religion or belief, age, or physical/mental
impairment.

- Performance reviews that are undertaken regularly, where goals set previously are appraised objectively. An employee should always know what expectations their line manager has of them, and what level of success they have achieved in fulfilling these expectations. There should be no shocks or surprises when it comes to the performance review.
- Training in proper recruitment and selection techniques for those engaged in these processes as well as training in equal opportunities issues is advisable. This is particularly important for line managers—and if you state in your policy that you will train all of them then you must see it through.

Defining your policy

Employers must have a clear, written policy that sets out in detail what they expect of their employees in terms of their attitude and behaviour. The policy should specify:

- the organisation's values in preventing discrimination
- the rights of all employees
- the individual and collective responsibilities of employees for preventing discrimination, bullying, and harassment
- the particular responsibilities of managers
- the extension of the policy to relationships with customers and other groups
- responsibilities for identifying and reporting breaches of the policy

■ what happens to those who breach policy—give it
teeth!

If you're looking at discrimination management afresh it will
be clear that you're not starting with a blank sheet. There
will be 'traditional' systems and ways of doing things in the
organisation that have evolved over the years. There might
also be—in larger organisations—an informal culture that
regulates relationships between people. This may be deeply
entrenched, and may also run counter to the evolving trends
in legislation to prevent discrimination.

There have been many examples in recent years of
corporate cultures that are (unwittingly) hostile to certain
groups of potential employees. Organisations are
increasingly being labelled as 'institutionally discriminatory'.

✔ Pay particular attention to understanding the full effects
of the informal culture in your workplace, and to ensuring
that it does not create problems. This is a difficult area: it
isn't easy to change established behaviours. You can
expect to come up against some resistance, which will
need sensitive handling.

Nor is this a problem that can simply be sorted in one go.
Organisational cultures and the social environment are
dynamic, changing systems, where people come and go,
and move across or up the organisation, building
relationships on their way. This means regular monitoring of
behaviour will be needed.

Defining your procedures

Clear, written procedures for reporting discrimination
and related problems should also be in place.
These should be visibly supported and followed
by managers and employee representatives.
The procedures should:

- be simple and understandable to all staff
- be positive, focusing clearly on resolving any problem
  as fast as possible
- contain sufficient step-by-step detail and guidance to
  encourage trust in its use by both 'victims' and
  concerned others
- be as short as reasonably possible, and contain
  target times for completion of each stage
- give guidance to those implementing it so that the
  same scrupulously fair decisions are applied in all
  comparable cases
- facilitate good record keeping

Step three: Know the rules

It is important to know that, as an employer, you're
responsible for the actions of your employees. Keeping
your employment practices within the law will protect
you from expensive litigation procedures and possible
payouts.

I The Equal Opportunities Code of Practice

The Equalities and Human Rights Commission will be publishing new codes of practice based on the Equality Act 2010. The current code of practice on equal opportunities makes three main recommendations:

- Each individual should be assessed according to his or her personal capability to carry out a given job. It should not be assumed that men only or women only will be able to perform certain kinds of work.
- Any entry qualifications or requirements which discourage applications from a gender group or deter married people must be justifiable in terms of the job to be done.
- Age limits should only be set if they are necessary for the job. Imposing an unjustifiable age limit could constitute unlawful indirect discrimination.

To comply with the recommendations, you will need to perform the following actions:

✔ Ensure that dismissal or redundancy policies are carefully and clearly drawn up, well publicised, and implemented.

✔ Maintain even-handed disciplinary procedures that don't tolerate unequal levels of performance between the gender groups.

✔ Offer voluntary redundancy to male and female employees on equal terms.

✓ If employment conditions should change as a result of a downturn in the market, make sure that working arrangements don't discriminate on the grounds of gender.

✓ Make provision for those who are physically or mentally impaired. This includes ensuring that non-hazardous access to the working and service areas is possible, and that any special furniture or equipment is available.

If an employer treats an able-bodied employee differently from a physically challenged employee, or does not make reasonable adjustments to enable a physically challenged person to work effectively, they are answerable to the law. 'Reasonable adjustments' would mean ensuring that features of the work environment did not put the disabled person at a disadvantage. This might entail being flexible about working hours and providing equipment, training, or assistance to remove the barriers that may otherwise prevent the person from being an effective employee. Remember that the test of reasonableness relates to the employer's ability to make adjustments, and so small businesses may be judged to have acted reasonably in some circumstances where much larger companies would have been expected to go further.

2 The Sex Discrimination Act

This Act makes it unlawful for any British employer to treat men and women differently when they are in comparable circumstances. It is also unlawful to engage in any form of harassment that may cause injury to the body or to the feelings of the employee.

Sexual harassment is usually taken to mean unwelcome physical, verbal, or non-verbal conduct of a sexual nature. This includes comments that the recipient finds demeaning or offensive (including comments about their appearance), intrusive questions about their sex life or sexual orientation, requests or demands for sexual favours, or any other behaviour that is intimidating, hostile, or humiliating.

✔ Don't assume that the absence of an objection means the behaviour is condoned or even acceptable. People sometimes try to put up with a situation for a while before taking action.

3 The Equal Pay Act

According to this Act, levels of pay and benefits must be set on the basis of the demands of the role and the value of the role to the business. These should be applied without prejudice to men or women. This means equal pay for equal jobs, and equal pay for jobs of equal value.

It also requires that regular salary and benefit reviews take place to ensure that the rationale for salary levels does not slip.

✔ Bear in mind that the Equality Act 2010 will make it unlawful for employers to include clauses in contracts of employment that prevent employees from discussing their pay or bonuses. The Act also gives the government the power to force private sector employers with 250 or more employees to publish information about differences in pay between male and female employees, although this will not happen before April 2013. However, it's worth taking steps now to get your house in order.

Step four: Introduce new policies appropriately

Initially, you need to focus the application of your discrimination policy on a few key HR procedures. This will help integrate your new approach to discrimination with the existing corporate environment.

Here are some of the places to start:

- **Recruitment**—recruit only on the basis of the skills and abilities needed to do the job.
- **Selection**—select on merit by focusing on objective information about skills, abilities, or potential. Seek evidence of positive attitudes to diversity in the workplace. If possible, publish your selection criteria and stay within them.
- **Promotion**—base promotion on the ability, or demonstrated potential, to do the job, and on appropriate behaviour defined by discrimination management policy.

- **Training and development**—encourage all employees, including part-time workers, to take advantage of relevant training opportunities, and show how the organisation offers development opportunities to all.
- **Redundancy**—base decisions on objective, communicated, job-related criteria to ensure the skills needed in the business are retained.
- **Retirement**—ensure that retirement schemes are fairly applied, taking individual and business needs into account.

Step five: Communicate

Keeping the channels of communication open between you and your employees is the single most effective way of avoiding discriminatory behaviour in the workplace. When people know what the rules are, and see that you're serious about implementing them, they will be less likely to risk contravening the employment acts.

As an ethical employer you should let your customers know your policies on creating a non-prejudicial environment for your employees. Increasingly, stakeholders are making ethical choices about whom they will or will not do business with.

Step six: Enjoy the benefits

Recent studies in Europe, the United States, and Australia have shown that attention to discrimination can produce tangible bottom-line benefits. Consultation between managers and employees about discrimination was found to demonstrate care and respect. By encouraging discussion of these issues, and showing willingness to incorporate good suggestions, you can build considerable loyalty among your employees.

Staff in the companies studied reported that:

- the atmosphere of the company became more positive and respectful
- taboos that prevented discussion of sensitive subjects were removed
- teamwork improved significantly
- employees discovered ways in which they could personally contribute to alleviating discrimination

On the other hand, organisations that paid little or no attention to discrimination were found to have:

- high absenteeism and turnover among those who felt they were victims of discrimination or harassment
- higher error and scrap rates
- increased accident rates, and higher claims for compensation
- low morale

- loss of reputation with customers
- lower productivity and quality
- more errors in making appointments to key positions

Common mistakes

✗ You don't provide clear company policies
Organisations sometimes forget to declare their attitude
towards equal opportunities until a case is brought
against them. Ignorance is no protection from the law,
and you must make sure that everyone is aware of your
policies.

✗ You are complacent
The most common mistake is being complacent or
unprepared—believing that 'it can't happen to us'.
When it does happen, however, the damage to
finances, profitability, and reputation can be very
severe. A secondary finding in one of the international
studies mentioned above was that, in some sectors,
almost 50% of employees thought that they had been
the victim of harassment, bullying, or discrimination.
Their employers were clearly not aware of this. That
is a huge number of potential lawsuits to be defended,
and fees and claims to be paid out.

✗ You don't change company culture
Professions that have been dominated by men are now
required to think about how to integrate women into
their traditionally male workforces. Many high-profile
cases have been brought against employers because

they haven't prepared for the entry of women into the profession. It's the responsibility of organisations to make sure that suitable practices are adopted to prevent any kind of discrimination.

✗ You think that only large organisations have to comply

Employment law doesn't take account of differences in the size of an organisation, its circumstances, or the market conditions. It is a common mistake for smaller businesses to ignore good employment practice with the excuse that they don't have the resources to support it.

STEPS TO SUCCESS

✔ Don't think it could never happen in your organisation.

✔ Have appropriate policies and procedures in place.

✔ Publicise your policies (internally and externally) and educate your employees. Always be clear.

✔ Enforce your policies, even in informal but work-related environments and keep up to date with the law.

Useful links

Acas (Advisory, Conciliation and Arbitration Service):
www.acas.co.uk
Equality and Human Rights Commission:
www.equalityhumanrights.com

Managing addictive behaviour

Drug and alcohol misuse is on the increase in the workplace and it can no longer be swept under the carpet. Working with an addicted colleague can be a nightmare for everyone involved. If you're suffering from an addiction yourself, it's important to deal with the problem early on, before it becomes an issue that could cost you your job.

Some companies are now instituting regular drug or breath tests as part of their standard conditions of employment. Given the statistics, this is understandable. Just look at the facts.

- Hangovers alone are estimated to cost UK industry between £53 million and £108 million each year.
- A survey conducted by Alcohol Concern in conjunction with the TUC suggests that one in four accidents happen as a result of alcohol misuse, and that around 40 million working hours are lost, costing an estimated £3 billion each year.
- The British Medical Association asserts that 60% of workplace fatalities are alcohol-related.

- **The Institute of Personnel and Development has published findings that suggest up to 21% of the workforce may be using drugs, the fastest growing group of users being young, high achievers who are turning to cocaine and ecstasy.**
- **A report issued by the Royal College of Physicians claims that drug addiction has risen fourfold in the past 10 years and that 25% of those seeking help for drug addiction are in employment.**
- **The Health and Safety Executive estimates that the cost to industry of drug abuse is £800 million per year.**

Step one: Spot the problem

Those who have alcohol or drug problems are likely to be identified through a number of telltale indicators. Their behaviour may appear erratic or out of character, they may take extended lunch breaks, or they may suddenly disappear without giving a reason at odd times throughout the day.

Many of us are familiar with the symptoms and consequences of heavy drinking, but drug problems are less widely understood and are therefore harder to recognise. Many of the telltale indicators of drug abuse aren't unlike those related to excessive consumption of alcohol.

Symptoms of drug abuse

These include:

- mood swings or uncharacteristic behaviour
- a tendency to become confused and irritable
- the development of problematical relationships
- a drop in work performance
- poor time-keeping and increased absenteeism

As a manager, if you observe these signals you may wish to arrange to meet for a performance review, during which you should concentrate on the behaviour you've observed and the likely reasons for these changes.

Step two: Do not dismiss the situation

The World Health Organization's European Charter on Alcohol states that ' . . . all people have the right to a family, community, and working life protected from accidents, violence, and other negative consequences of alcohol consumption'.

✔ Never ignore a colleague's addiction or assume that there is nothing you can do. Early intervention will only be of benefit. Alcohol and drug misuse not only affect the individual concerned, but also endanger the circle of people surrounding them, and have the potential to destroy the person's career and relationships.

✔ Do not underestimate the damaging effects of drink—for the individual and for your organisation. There is no question that alcohol reduces the ability to make sound judgments or decisions and increases the likelihood of mistakes through the loss of spatial awareness and control of the body. As heavy drinkers or drug users become more unreliable and their behaviour and judgment more erratic, their productivity diminishes and accidents become more likely.

TOP TIP

Every organisation should have an alcohol policy to provide clear guidelines for dealing with alcohol misuse at work. This policy will assure that those with alcohol problems will be treated considerately and will be encouraged to seek help. The policy should be developed with the input of senior and middle managers and agreed by employees and their representatives.

Step three: Publish the policy

Many organisations now operate a workplace alcohol and drug policy that encourages sobriety and freedom from drugs. In spite of such initiatives, the International

Labour Organization estimates that, globally, 3–5% of the average workforce is alcohol dependent, and that up to 25% drinks heavily enough to be at risk of dependence.

Prevention is always better than cure. Much can be done from an organisational perspective to raise awareness of drug and alcohol issues, so if you're a manager and you have a policy addressing these problems, make sure that everyone knows about it. Follow these steps:

✔ Post drug and alcohol information prominently in the office or on your intranet (if you have one) and embark on an education programme to ensure that everyone is aware of the issues.

✔ Outline the potential health and safety dangers to users and their colleagues. Explain that the organisation sees drug and alcohol misuse in the same light as any other illness, and that it will be treated in the same way. Early identification of employees at risk should be encouraged.

✔ Publish the rules about alcohol consumption and drug use at work, and ensure that the message is clearly displayed in places where employees enter the business and where people gather together.

✔ Offer advice and assistance to those who feel they have a problem, and outline the help that is available. This could be through a combination of external and internal resources: there are a wide range of support services available, from medical assistance to support groups and counselling services.

✔ Ensure confidentiality for anyone who seeks advice or assistance.

✔ Publish guidelines for disciplinary procedures and make clear what provision will be made for sick leave for treatment.

✔ Outline the basis on which an individual may return to the same job after treatment, and what level of tolerance exists for repeated leave for treatment. Termination of employment may occur on the grounds of ill health if treatment is deemed to be unsuccessful.

✔ Make sure that a regular review of the organisation's stance on drug and alcohol misuse is carried out and that the policy document is periodically updated.

Some organisations have a policy of running screening programmes prior to a final recruitment decision; others periodically repeat these during employment. These types of checks are especially important if the company's products, services, or methods are highly confidential, characterised by complex processes, or performed in an environment where physical safety can be an issue.

TOP TIP
Employers are not currently compelled by law to implement alcohol or drug policies, but Health and Safety legislation demands that they provide and maintain a safe working environment. If incidents occur as a result of alcohol or drug abuse, both employer and employee could be liable under this legislation. Employment law requires employers to treat dependency as a form of sickness. This definition enables the employee to seek treatment to overcome the problem.

Step four: Act sensitively

The people who suffer most—and who notice the problem first—are always those closest to the misuser. It is therefore likely that, if you encounter this problem, the individual concerned will be a friend or close colleague. You might prefer to talk to them on a personal level before addressing matters in a professional context. If you decide to broach the subject, do so with extreme tact. The individual is likely to react defensively to your concern, and you must not become too embroiled yourself.

✔ If you witness a friend or colleague drinking excessively or under the influence of drugs, intervene. This may be a simple action such as calling a taxi to take the person home. Although this may feel intrusive, at least it won't result in any physical damage being done.

✔ Try talking to your friend when they have returned to full control to find out if they are aware that they may have a problem and ask them if you can help.

✔ Offer support, but avoid the role of counsellor. Helping someone manage an addiction requires professional expertise. The journey to recovery is often rocky, and by taking on too much responsibility you could jeopardise a good friendship.

✔ Talk to your colleague's manager or to the human resources department. Don't think of it as being sneaky or telling tales but as a sign of concern for his or her welfare.

TOP TIP

If you suspect a team member's work is suffering because of problems with alcohol, arrange a meeting with them to share your concerns. Do not mention your suspicions at this stage; rather give the person an opportunity to allay your fears without becoming defensive. You could explore possible work-related causes to see if you can elicit an explanation that puts your mind at rest. Failing this you may want to discuss the organisation's alcohol policy and offer further assistance.

Common mistakes

✗ **You leave it too long before taking action**

Tackling substance misuse is difficult, and many people leave it too long before taking action. Avoiding the problem only makes the situation worse for the individual and his or her colleagues, so it's important not to let things drift on. Besides, inaction sends a powerful message to others, who may overindulge because they believe that the organisation doesn't take substance misuse seriously. If you're a manager dealing with an individual, ask for an interim performance review meeting and explore the reasons behind the behaviours you've observed. Once these are out in the open, the next logical step is to provide the right kind of help.

✗ **You don't call in professional help**

Being a supportive friend to drug or alcohol misusers may not serve them well in the long run and is no substitute for professional help. Dealing with addiction is a complicated business and should be facilitated by a trained counsellor. There may be someone in the human resources department (if you have one), who has experience of this form of counselling, but there are also many high-quality external resources that can assist.

✗ **You fail to provide a clear policy**

Organisations often don't consider drawing up an alcohol or drug policy until they actually have to deal with someone for whom drugs or alcohol have become a problem. As these forms of addiction are becoming increasingly commonplace, it's a good idea to ensure everything is in place to deal with the problem.

STEPS TO SUCCESS

✔ Have a widely published policy on substance misuse *before* problems arise.

✔ Don't accuse a colleague of addictive behaviour without investigating other possibilities first—there may be a more innocent explanation.

✔ Remember that addiction is an illness and should be treated as such.

✔ Never ignore addictive behaviour. The longer it goes on, the more of a problem it becomes for everyone.

✔ Bring in professional help at the earliest opportunity—don't try to counsel the individual without proper training.

Useful links

Drinksense:

www.drinksense.org

Hazards:

www.hazards.org/haz77/drugsandalcohol.pdf

Health and Safety Executive (alcohol and drugs at work):

www.hse.gov.uk/alcoholdrugs

7
Managing poor performance

Given the cost of recruitment, it's always worth trying to help an individual to develop from poor to acceptable performance. Effective management of results—particularly from poor performers—is crucial. However, it can feel awkward or embarrassing to discuss a team member's weaknesses, so such issues can sometimes go unchecked until they affect the rest of the business. This chapter will help you to end poor performance nightmares before they begin.

Reasons for poor performance

Poor performance can result from many causes, including:

- inability to manage perception or pressure
- failure to prioritise
- lack of skill, knowledge, or motivation
- conflict of personalities or styles
- over-promotion (often termed 'the Peter Principle'), where the person is actually out of his or her depth
- lack of resources, support, or co-operation from others

67

■ change in performance management systems or
processes

Step one: Use performance management systems

Frequently, by the time the poor performance has been identified, the damage has already been done. Prevention is better than cure, so establishing performance management systems—structured methods of identifying and improving poor performance—is ideal. These require that each individual has clear objectives, understands how these affect others, is aware of what is needed to deliver the objectives, and is confident of having the necessary skills and experience.

✔ Put these systems in place *before* problems ever arise. It will save considerable management time and worry.

TOP TIP
Sales teams are very results-oriented, and poor performers are quickly identified. Some theories about running sales teams suggest that you constantly churn the bottom group of performers, separating the wheat from the chaff. Managing poor performance can be highly time-consuming, particularly when

---

you want to be spending time supporting
stronger performers. The first step is to
make sure that you understand why this
group is consistently failing to meet its
targets. Then you need to set clear
and attainable goals and monitor its
progress at regular intervals. Finally,
make sure that you're prepared to
manage the consequences if team
members continue to underperform.

Step two: Define poor performance

Poor performance is defined by a range of factors. It's
important that a manager can decipher which are
conduct issues and which are capability/competence
issues, as each may require a different course of
action.

Conduct	Capability/Competence
■ Lateness, absenteeism	■ Failure to carry out tasks reasonably
■ Attitude	
■ Bad language	■ Failure to perform duties to an adequate standard
■ Sex/racial discrimination	
	■ Failure to provide high standards of customer care
■ Negligence or abuse of company property	■ Unsatisfactory references
■ Abusive behaviour to colleagues, managers, or customers	■ Infringement of regulations
	■ Failure to observe company policies and procedures

Step three: Follow disciplinary procedure

Your organisation must act with consistency and fairness and, where possible, be able to show that it has provided guidelines and coaching to achieve the desired actions and behaviour from its staff.

If a performance problem fails to be resolved, you may need to follow a disciplinary procedure. Here are a few useful guidelines.

✔ Carry out a full investigation and ensure that all evidence is well documented.

✔ Hold a formal hearing. Make sure the employee is given written notice of it. The employee is entitled to representation.

✔ Review all evidence. Formally outline the disciplinary action to be taken.

✔ Consider separating out conduct and capability issues, as many organisations do when undertaking disciplinary action. In the case of capability, the employee is given two chances to improve. However, if the problem is one of conduct, the process is less lenient. It is important to build in time to improve as part of the disciplinary process.

In any situation, prevention is the preferred option. However, where this isn't possible the manager needs to:

- be fair and unbiased at all times
- behave consistently
- pay personal attention to the matter
- understand whether it's a conduct or capability issue
- work within the guidelines and procedures if it reaches the stage of disciplinary action
- recognise the importance of training and guidance

Step four: Take preventative measures

An important part of building a team is ensuring that everyone is in a role that matches their skills and that each team member knows what they are trying to achieve. This should minimise the problem of poor performance.

✔ Communicate clearly. Leaders need to make explicit the goals of the business; managers need to break these down so that individuals understand how their targets relate to the overall business, and therefore how important their contribution is.

✔ Don't over-promote people. Just because someone does a great job at one level does not necessarily mean that they can tackle the next level.

✔ Ensure that managers are spending time with individuals to identify areas of risk before they affect performance.

✔ Don't overestimate goals and objectives. Optimistic management can be detrimental.

✔ Be aware of the culture of the business and ensure that goals are set appropriately.

TOP TIP

Restructuring can adversely affect individual performance. People often take time to adjust to new situations, and some cope with change better than others. If someone you manage is struggling with the switch, talk to him or her and explore exactly what differences the change has made to their working life. This kind of problem often emerges when communication is poor, which can make it difficult for someone to prioritise or understand what needs to be done—as well as to feel they have no support. You may need to help build the necessary new relationships, provide more support, and be clear on priorities.

Step five: Monitor your own performance

It's all very well dealing with other people's failings—but what about your own? Sometimes, you may need to admit that you're not doing as well as you could be. An honest examination of your performance might well reveal areas for improvement.

✔ Establish your limits. Where you feel that you don't have the skills, experience, or knowledge to achieve the objectives set for you, ask for help before it becomes a performance management issue.

✔ Try to understand why you haven't met the objectives. What support would help you improve your performance? If the goals aren't clear, ask for them to be redefined so that you can work towards them and manage the expectations of others.

✔ Consider your attitude. How do others react to your behaviour? Remember that what works in one culture doesn't always move easily to others. *How* you say something is as important as *what* you say. Try to identify friction points before they become serious performance issues.

✔ Monitor your level of motivation. We can often outgrow roles, or find we need different challenges to feel rewarded. Work with your boss or senior colleagues to understand why you feel unmotivated. What type of recognition or appreciation would help? Explore whether the pressures in the role have changed, or whether you have different life goals. Sometimes when our circumstances change, the expectation we have of ourselves also changes. Remember that it's more

cost-effective for organisations to re-motivate and
align an existing employee than to recruit, train, and
develop a new one, so your managers will want to
keep you.

Common mistakes

✗ You overreact and ignore external factors

When you deal with poor performance, remain
unbiased, fair, and consistent. Always explore why
it has occurred and what could have contributed to
it. Is it part of a pattern, or is it a one-off situation
that is likely to be easily resolved? Overreacting to
situations isn't good for the employee, for you, or
for the organisation.

✗ You set the bar too high and objectives aren't explicit

It's important, when setting goals, to make sure that
they are clearly defined and achievable. Remember that
different people have different capabilities. Check that
your expectations fit with the culture of the business
(some businesses have cultures where expectations
are set higher than reality—so failing to meet explicit
goals is forgiven). Set clear, short process milestones,
so that you can quickly recognise where performance
may slip. Most important of all, communicate regularly.
Performance targets discussed at the beginning of the
year and then measured at the end may not be
appropriate for everyone.

✗ You do not address poor performance early enough

Performance needs to be measurable. The easier it is to measure, the easier it is to manage. Checks need to be made at regular intervals to understand how close an individual is to achieving, or not achieving, targets. Schedule regular reviews and encourage employees to monitor their own performance. Ask them to rate their progress and suggest ways in which they could improve. Managers often set objectives and leave people to it — but if the goals aren't met, it can be critical for the business. Good performance management ensures that possible failure is identified early on and the risk managed appropriately.

✗ You expect instant results from a series of coaching sessions

If someone is performing poorly, it's not usually appropriate simply to prescribe coaching and hope for the best. Coaching isn't a magic wand for turning poor performers into good performers — it's better used as a proactive tool to develop a potentially good performer. Confirm first that the individual has the capability to fulfil their role, then identify what needs to be done to help them succeed. Coaching in this context is then positive and motivational. Often, it's a good idea to give new role holders increasingly demanding performance measures until they have settled in. Always make sure you build in a fair amount of time for the employee to make the necessary improvements.

✗ You confuse personality clashes with poor performance

Where issues may be personality-driven, bring in an impartial third party to 'referee'. Separate out the issues and look at different ways of dealing with them. Resolving one may well have knock-on effects on the others. In some cases poor performance may be a perceived rather than a real problem. This can happen when there is a difference in understanding between a manager and his or her subordinate: they may each go about tasks differently, but no less effectively.

STEPS TO SUCCESS

✔ Measure performance at all times—and make sure every team member knows what constitutes good and bad performance.

✔ Set clear and achievable targets, offer feedback.

✔ Match people to their roles. Don't expect coaching to turn an unsuitable person into a top performer.

Useful links

OneClickHR.com:
www.oneclickhr.com/?hrguide/article.asp?article=108
PerformMAX:
www.manageperformance.com

Thinking around problems

New ways of thinking can help you solve problems before they become nightmares. It is estimated that human beings only use 10% of their brain capacity, so clearly we have vast untapped thinking potential. Exercising the brain in a variety of new ways allows us to expand into those unused capacities.

Our thinking styles develop over the years and become habitual—particularly those we form as we pass through the education system, which tend to focus on the skills of analysis. So when people make statements like 'I'm not creative', or 'I'm not really a thinker', all this means is that they haven't been introduced to, or adopted, different ways of using their minds.

A situation only seems nightmarish when you can't see a way round it. A more open-minded approach could give you a simple solution.

Can one process solve every problem?
In most situations, it's a good idea to allow people to understand problems and then solve them in their own way. However, using tried and tested techniques of problem-

solving—ones that are plainly mapped out and used uniformly—allows others to understand the problem and the areas being explored. The process ensures that everyone involved has the opportunity to actively participate in solving the problem at any stage.

While problems *are* always different, there are some common approaches and processes for solving them. Problems can be diagnosed and the various elements identified, whether you're talking about problems in the post-room, a manufacturing roadblock, or an IT systems failure.

The key is to think *before* you act. The best way to turn a minor problem into a major nightmare is to implement a solution without thinking through the implications.

Step one: Identify the problem

Understanding a problem requires an ability to see it in its entirety—in breadth, depth, and context. Here are a number of ways to evaluate the scope of a problem:

- **Recognition**—can you see or feel the problem? Is it isolated, or part of a bigger problem?
- **Symptoms**—how is it showing itself?
- **Causes**—why has it happened?
- **Effects**—what else is being affected by it?

The task then is to break the main problem down into smaller problems, in order to determine whether you're the right person or team to handle it. If not, you need to transfer the problem-solving process to those better equipped to deal with it. If the answer is yes, ask additional questions, including: Do you have the right resources? What are some of the obstacles? What is the anticipated benefit? Once you get answers, move on to the next step.

Step two: Gather data

There are two important questions here: what do you need to know, and how are you going to get it? Most information can be accessed, but there are often time and resource issues involved in this process. Data collection involves investigating the symptoms, the underlying causes, and/or the overall effects of the problem. Each may have different implications as to how the problem is viewed. Data-gathering techniques include:

- workflow analysis
- surveys and questionnaires
- flow charts
- group and/or one-to-one interviews

Step three: Think systematically

With the mass of information available these days, the following techniques can be useful to determine what is important and how best to make sense of it.

1 SWOT analysis

This is used to identify strengths and weaknesses and to examine the existing opportunities and threats. Answering questions in each of the four areas enables you to think systematically about a problem and potential solutions. Say, for example, your main headache at work was about the launching of a new product in a tricky market. The SWOT analysis could work as follows:

Strengths: What are some advantages of your new product that the public has been seeking? What are the features that distinguish it from rival products?

Weaknesses: Where are the areas of vulnerability? Is the price a barrier?

What could be improved? Would different product features make it better?

What are the known vulnerabilities in the market? Is the product launch time-sensitive?

Opportunities: Where are the opportunities in terms of technology, markets, policy, and social trends?

Have you got a new commercial idea or found a new way of doing things?

Can you capitalise on what rivals did wrong?

Threats: What barriers do you face? Is your target market right?

Are you facing a change in regulations?

Should you wait until it's official? Is the
competition stealing a march on you?
Are there threats to your financial
situation? Should you try to raise money
now, or wait for a better time?

2 Decision trees

Decision trees allow decisions to be made in situations
where there is a great deal of information to sift through.
They create a framework in which you can examine
alternative solutions and their impact.

✔ Start your decision tree on one side of a piece of paper,
with a symbol representing the decision to be made.
Different lines representing various solutions open out
like a fan from this nexus. Additional decisions or
uncertainties that need to be resolved are indicated on
these lines and, in turn, form the new decision point,
from which yet more options fan out.

3 Critical path analysis

This is another way of approaching complex projects. It
allows you to determine when certain activities should be
completed, so that a project may finish on time and on
budget. The essential concept behind it is that some
activities are dependent on others being completed first
(sequential), and others may be completed more or less
at any time (parallel). The ordering of these activities creates
the critical path through the project.

4 Mind maps

Developed by Tony Buzan, these are graphical tools used to represent whatever is on your mind. They help you get everything down on paper, with no initial emphasis on ordering or prioritising. They could be a useful first step in seeing how the land lies and identifying throughways.

✔ Start with a circle on a large sheet of paper. Inside the circle put the word or picture that best represents the idea you wish to explore. Then place other words—perhaps in smaller circles—around the hub. Let your mind wander, and bring in a galaxy of associated words and images. Finally, connect the circles with lines, accenting similar themes with colours or symbols. Once everything is down, you can study how the various 'satellites' relate to the hub, and how you want to apply the content to your personal goals.

Step four: Think creatively

Techniques that extend our thinking into the more creative realms include:

1 Brainstorming

This is a well-known technique for generating options, where every idea submitted is treated positively. This 'anything goes' approach often stimulates the presentation of viable ideas that wouldn't otherwise have been thought of. It is only in the final stages, when all ideas have been collected, that the honing and prioritising process begins.

TOP TIP

In meetings where brainstorming isn't part of the agenda, there often isn't time to indulge someone's creative effort. However, people who come up with off-the-wall suggestions may get frustrated if you have to rein them in. Explain what kind of thinking you're looking for in that particular setting, and offer them another context in which they can freewheel helpfully. Many companies have research and development departments that encourage off-the-wall thinking.

---

2 Questioning

✔ Ask why a problem is occurring, and then ask again— four more times. This allows you to drill down and get to the heart of the matter.

✔ Alternatively, ask the six universal questions to explore the full extent of a problem: What? Where? When? How? Why? Who?

3 Six thinking hats

This is a powerful technique developed by lateral thinking pioneer, Edward de Bono.

✔ Allocate each individual a series of imaginary hats, which represent different outlooks, according to colour. This forces people to move into different modes of thinking. White hats focus on the data, look for gaps, extrapolate from history, and examine future trends. Red hats use intuition and emotion to look at problems. Black hats look at the negative, and find reasons why something may not work. If an idea can get through this process, it's more likely to succeed. Yellow hats think positively. This hat helps you to see the benefits of a decision. Green hats develop creative, freewheeling solutions. There is no room for criticism in this mode; it's strictly positive. Blue hats orchestrate the meeting—you're in control in this hat. Feel free to propose a new hat to keep ideas flowing.

Step five: Weigh up potential solutions

Taking time to identify the most appropriate solution from your range of options is very important. Suggestions need to be winnowed down to a shortlist, containing only the most realistic possibilities. To do this, set some hard measures.

✔ Try to determine the costs and benefits of the suggested solutions. If, for example, you feel that outside investment is needed to solve a particular problem, work out the payback period. You can then assess whether your senior management team will accept it.

✔ Analyse each potential solution in turn. Force field analysis is useful for this. By looking at the forces that will support or challenge a decision (such as finances or market conditions), you can strengthen the pros and diminish the cons. Draw three columns, and place the situation or issue in the middle. The pros push on one side, and the cons push on the other. Allocate scores to each force to convey its potency. This allows you to measure the overall advantages and disadvantages of any given action.

The chosen solution needs to meet some key criteria. Do you have the necessary people, money, and time to achieve it? Will you get a sufficient return on investment? Is the solution acceptable to others involved in the situation? Draw up:

- a rationale of why you've reached your particular conclusion
- a set of criteria to judge the solution's success
- a plan of action and contingencies
- a schedule for implementation
- a team to carry out, be responsible for, and approve the solution

Step six: Put the chosen solution into action

Implementation means having action plans with relevant deadlines and contingencies built in. Any implementation needs constant review, and the implementation team

needs to make sure it has the support of relevant
management. Keep asking:

- Are deadlines being met?
- Are team members happy, and is communication strong
  within and from the team?
- Has the team been recognised for its achievements?
- Are the improvements measurable?
- Is the situation reviewed regularly?

Step seven: Measure success

All experience can be valuable in terms of adding in-house
knowledge and expertise. So ask yourself two important
questions:

- How well did it work?
- What did we learn from the process?

✓ Think of creating a case study that can be shared with
others—either at a conference or directly.

✓ Canvass people's opinions regarding the effectiveness
of the process and its outcome. Ask for improvements
that could be incorporated into a second phase.

✓ Don't be scared of involving your clients in any
evaluation; this can convey a positive message if
handled properly, and builds trust in your ability to
troubleshoot problems and implement solutions.

Common mistakes

✗ You tackle too large a problem
Don't take on problems that lie beyond the control of
the team. People often tackle problems that are too
general—focus on what is specific and achievable.

✗ You assume everyone thinks like you do
To be productive in groups, you need a diverse range
of ways of contributing. Look around you at work;
you'll recognise different thinking styles and recall how
those have led to better clarity decisions and outcomes.

✗ You are critical of others' creativity
Under pressure, it's easy to think: 'The last thing I need is
flaky ideas when I've got a deadline!' But when you're
not stressed, you've probably seen the immense value
that creativity can bring. Try not to stifle creative thought;
rather, guide and control it openly.

✗ You get too used to a lack of structure
Entrepreneurial businesses are often formed as a result
of an extraordinarily creative mind. However, focused
thinking and systems thinking will be necessary for good
decision-making and management.

✗ You get carried away by the process
Often, when running workshops, the process becomes
more important than the ideas and intellectual
discussion: understanding the problem and finding
imaginative solutions requires strong facilitation.

STEPS TO SUCCESS

✓ Remember that a 'nightmare' is just a problem for which you haven't yet found a solution. Analyse the situation and determine what is important by looking at strengths and weaknesses and examining existing opportunities and threats.

✓ Explore alternative solutions by using graphic representations, like decision trees and mind maps.

✓ Extend your thinking into the more creative realms by brainstorming; fostering different perspectives and points of attack and; questioning why a problem is occurring.

✓ In a group, let each member take on a different outlook to force new modes of thinking: emotional, positive, negative, creative, and factual.

✓ Assess the impact of the solution and identify areas for improvement in your problem-solving processes.

Useful links

Edward de Bono's website:
www.edwdebono.com
Innovative thinking resources for entrepreneurs:
www.innovationtools.com
ThinkBuzan.com:
www.thinkbuzan.com/uk

Where to find more help

The Equal Opportunities Handbook: How to Deal with Everyday Issues of Unfairness 4th ed
Phil Clements, Tony Spinks
London: Kogan Page, 2009
240pp ISBN: 0749452978
This is a plainly written resource for students, managers, trainers, human resource management staff, teachers, and all those with an interest in equality of opportunity. It sets out straightforward procedures to guide fair, courteous, and sensitive behaviour to others, and includes a summary of recent legislation and agencies, self-assessment sections, and ways of identifying and preventing institutional discrimination.

Survive bullying at work: How to stand up for yourself and take control
Lorenza Clifford
London: A & C Black, 2006
96pp ISBN: 0713675209
This book covers everything from understanding why bullies behave as they do, to standing up for yourself and knowing your rights at work. Whether you are being bullied yourself or want to help a victim of bullying, this guide provides essential information that can help everyone move on with their lives.

Managing Workplace Bullying
Aryanne Oade
Basingstoke: Palgrave Macmillan, 2009
192pp ISBN: 0230228089
A comprehensive and practical book designed to help you recognise bullying behaviour at work and identify and select inter-personal strategies for handling it.